PREHISTORIC
ACTUAL
SIZE

STEVE JENKINS

"Morgan's tooth"
200 million years ago
10-centimetre-long body

F

FRANCES LINCOLN
CHILDREN'S BOOKS

Velociraptor (vee-*lohs*-i-*rap*-tor) was a swift, agile predator that may have been covered with feathers.

75 million years ago
2 metres long

Animals have lived on earth for hundreds of millions of years. Dragonflies the size of seagulls, meat-eating dinosaurs bigger than a bus, giant flying reptiles, fierce predatory birds over two metres tall – they all appeared, thrived for millions of years, and then died out as the world changed around them. In this book you'll see what these prehistoric animals, along with many others, may have looked like at **actual size.**

One of the first animals to appear on Earth was a tiny, hard-shelled **protozoan** (pro-toh-*zoh*-an). It was almost too small to see.

550 million years ago

1 millimetre across

The sharp-eyed **sea scorpion** hunted in shallow seas.

420 million years ago
2 metres long

The tiny **spiny shark,** one of the first fish, was protected by armour plates and sharp spines.

410 million years ago

8 centimetres long

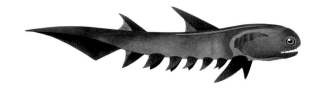

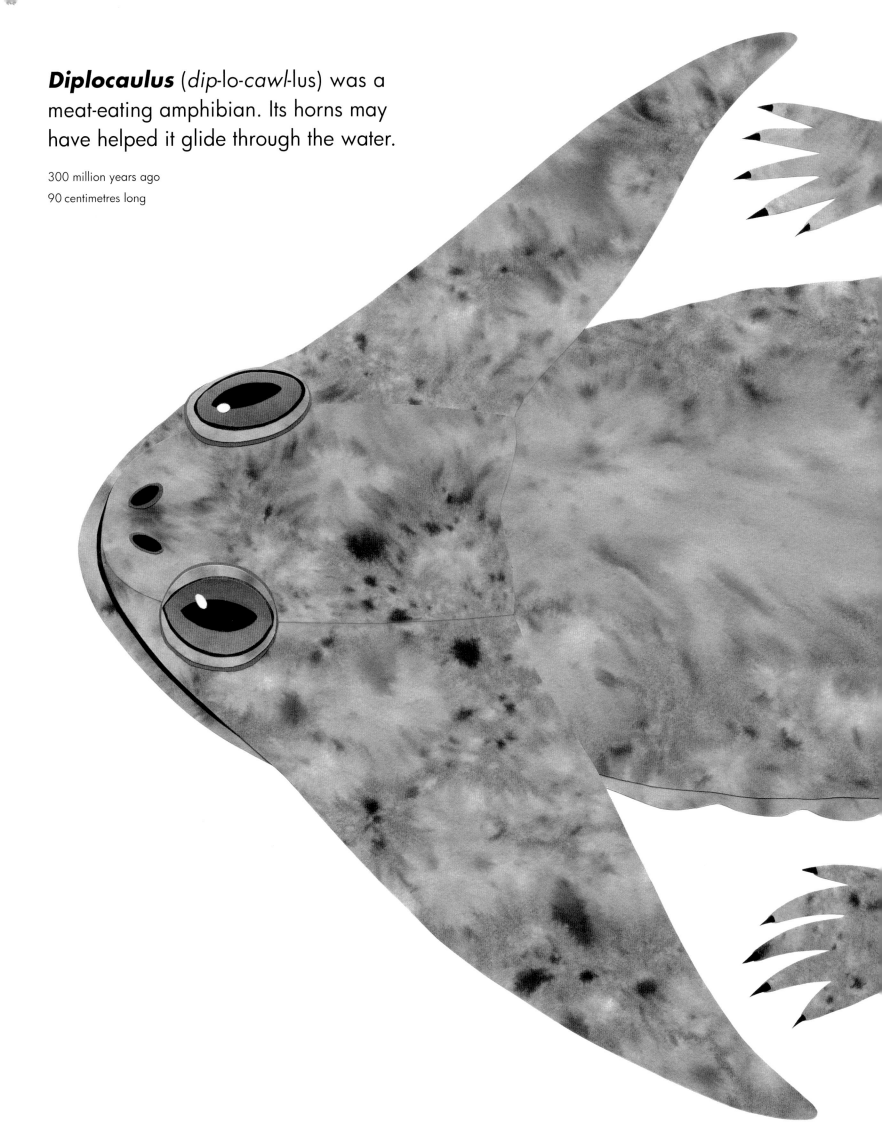

Diplocaulus (*dip*-lo-*cawl*-lus) was a meat-eating amphibian. Its horns may have helped it glide through the water.

300 million years ago

90 centimetres long

Imagine a **dragonfly** with wings more than 60 centimetres across!

300 million years ago
69-centimetre wingspan

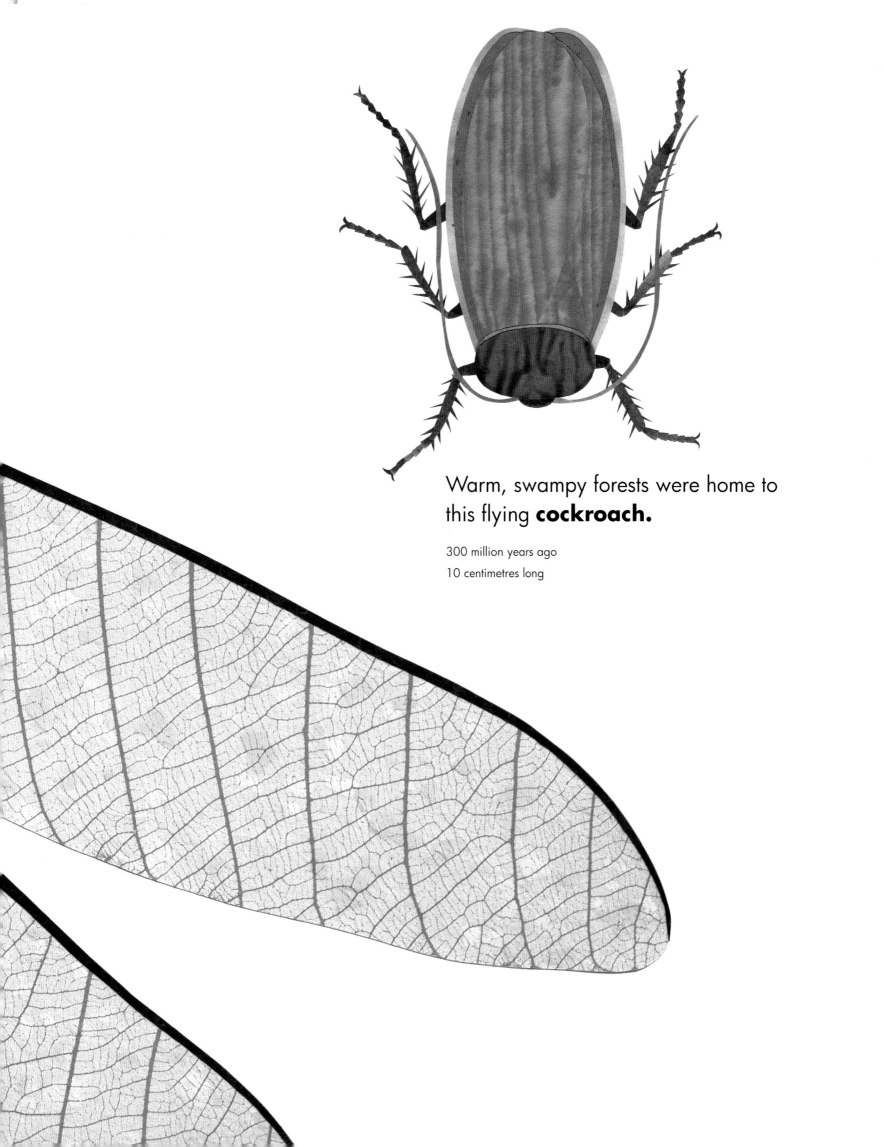

Warm, swampy forests were home to
this flying **cockroach.**

300 million years ago
10 centimetres long

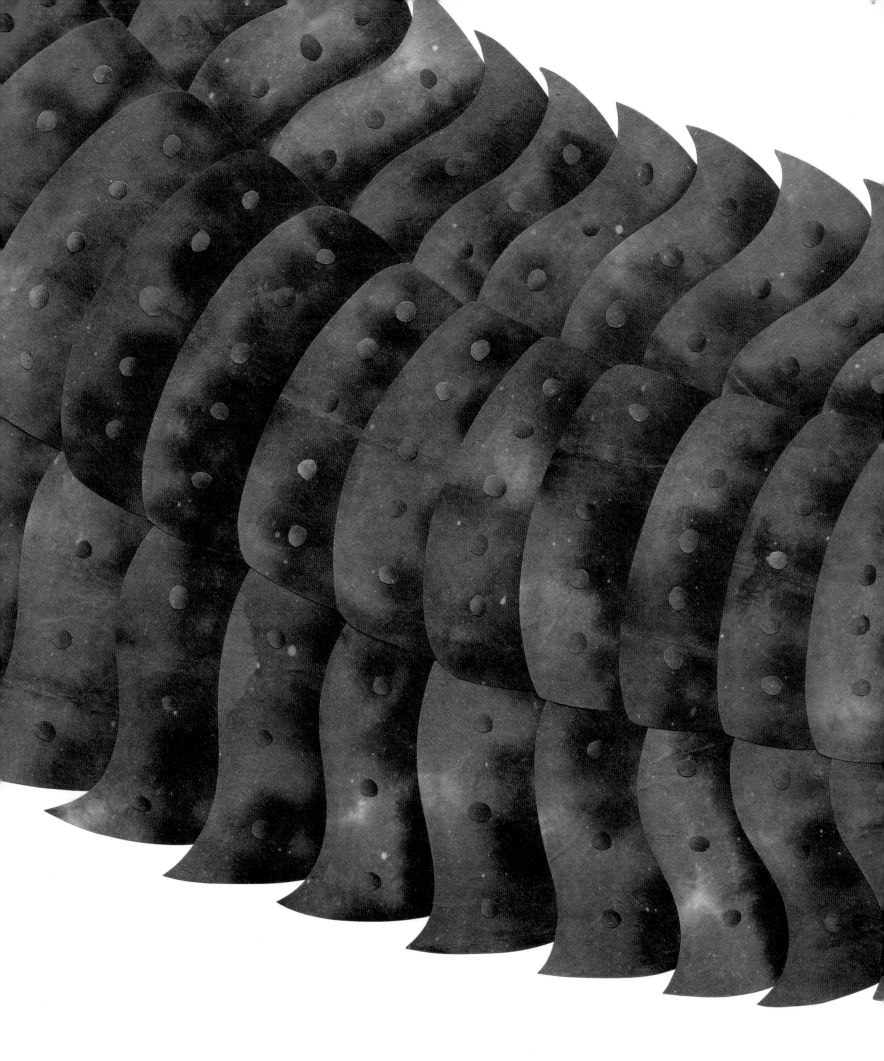

This giant **millipede** had as many as thirty pairs of legs.

300 million years ago
2 metres long

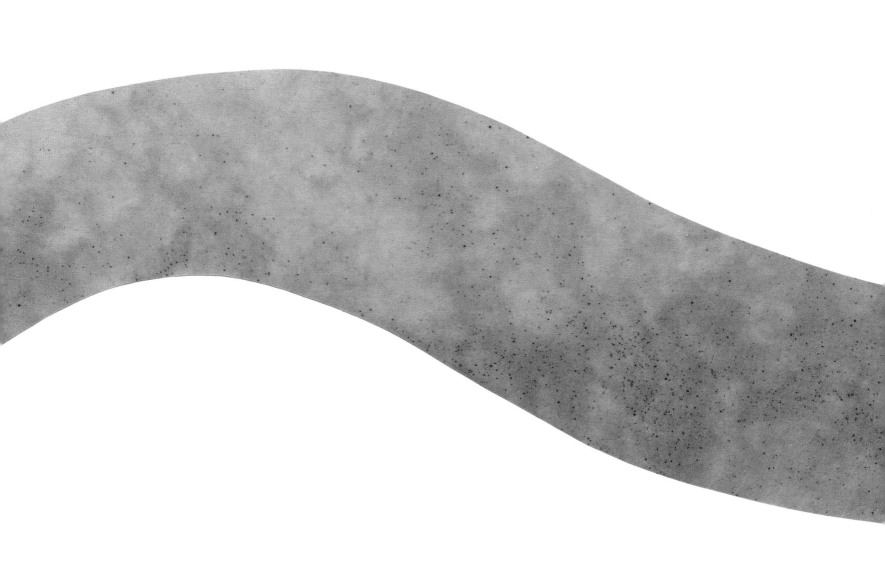

Despite its name, **Dinocephalosaurus**
(*di*-no-*sef*-ah-lo-*sawr*-us) wasn't a dinosaur.
It was a fish-eating reptile that sucked
up its prey by quickly stretching out its
long neck.

230 million years ago
2½ metres long

The bird-like **Saltopus** (*salt*-oh-pus), one of the smallest dinosaurs, was a swift runner.

210 million years ago
60 centimetres long

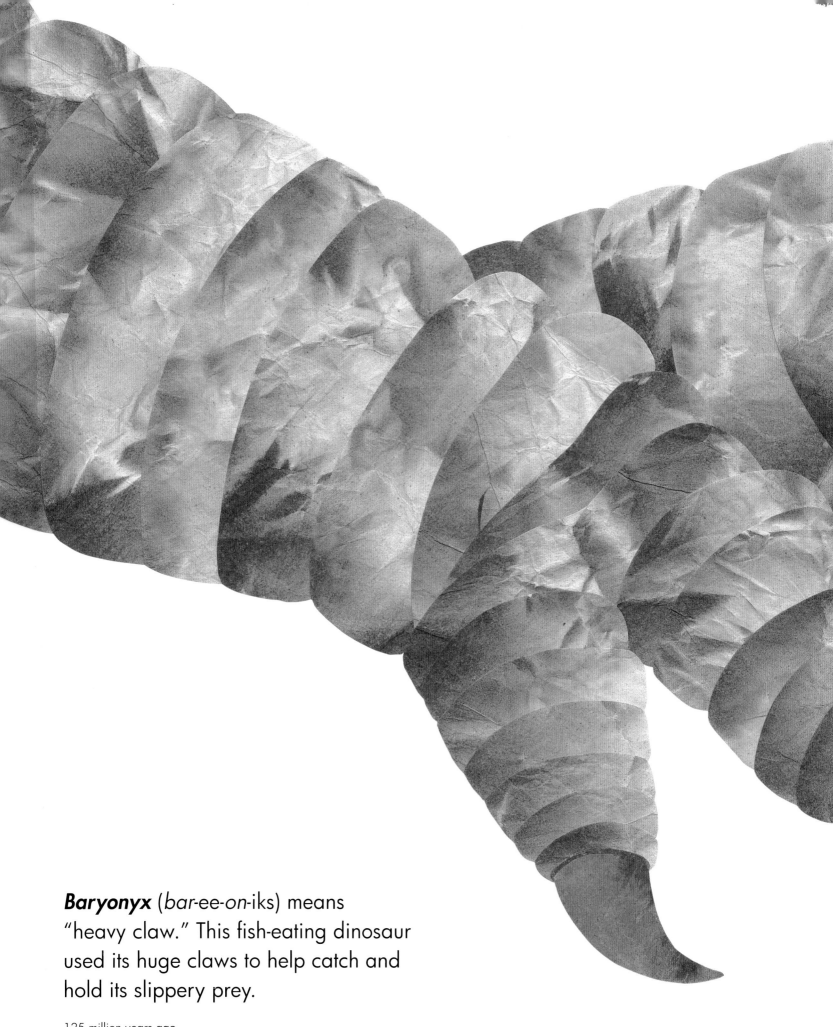

Baryonyx (*bar-ee-on*-iks) means "heavy claw." This fish-eating dinosaur used its huge claws to help catch and hold its slippery prey.

125 million years ago

10 metres long

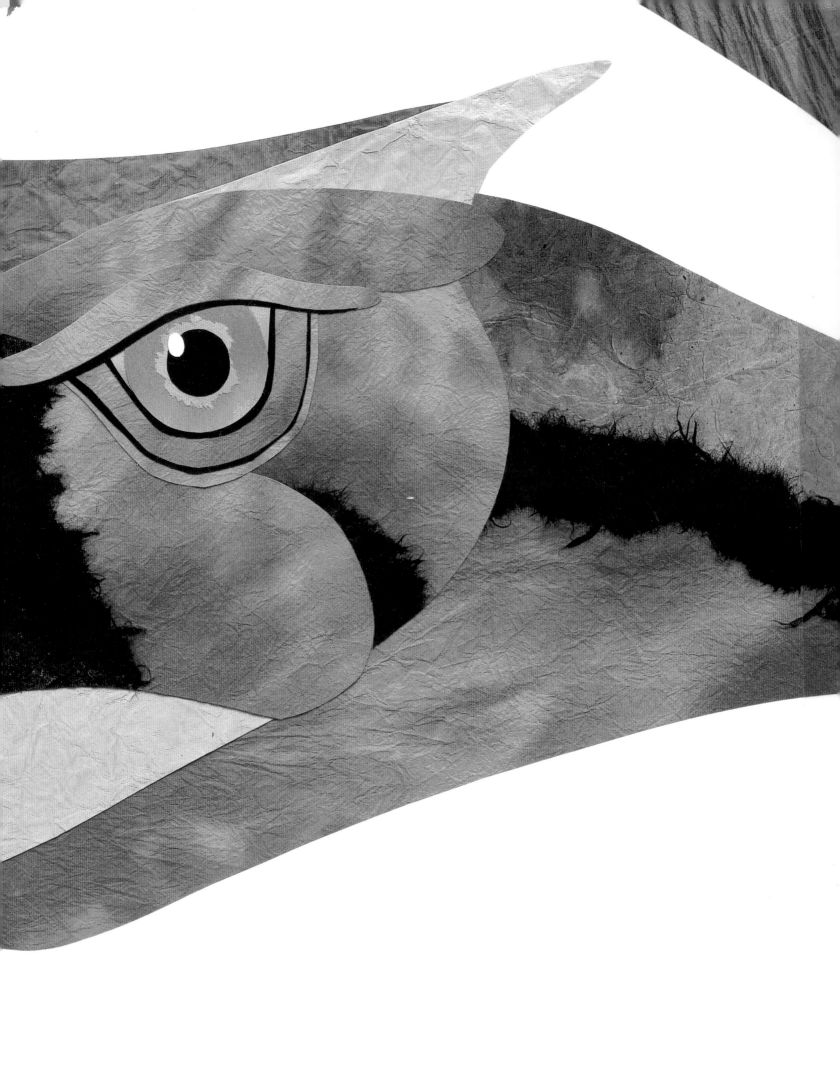

Dsungaripterus (*jung*-ah-*rip*-ter-us) was a flying reptile. It may have used its upturned beak to pry open and eat shellfish.

135 million years ago
3-metre wingspan

Giganotosaurus (jig-an-not-o-sawr-us)
may have been the largest predator that
ever lived on land.

100 million years ago
14 metres long

Protoceratops (*pro*-toh-*ser*-a-tops)
was a plant-eating dinosaur that used its
sharp beak to bite through tough stems
and leaves. A baby *Protoceratops* was
only about 15 centimetres long when
it hatched.

80 million years ago
180 centimetres long

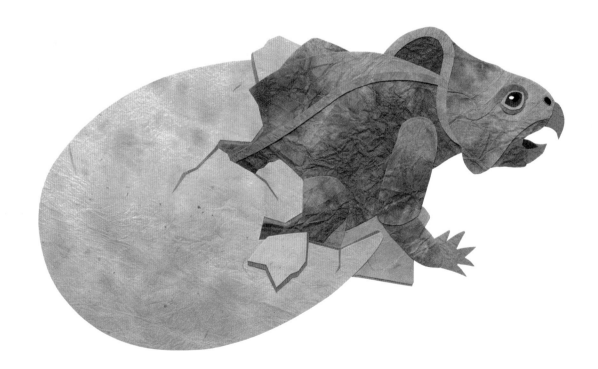

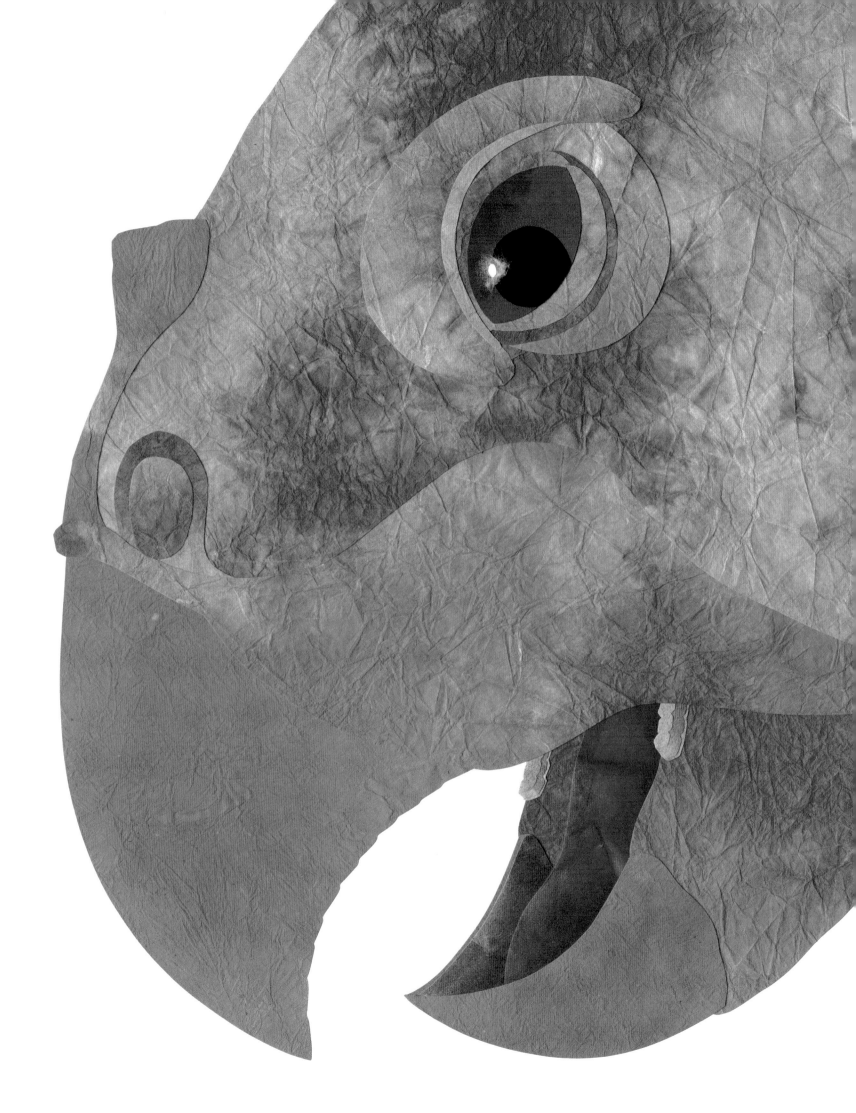

Leptictidium (*lep*-tik-*tid*-ee-um), an insect-eating mammal, hopped about on its back legs.

45 million years ago

60 centimetres long

The **terror bird** lived in South America.
It was the largest predator of its time –
big enough to eat a horse.

3 million years ago
2½ metres tall

How do we know what prehistoric animals looked like? Fossils, which preserve the form of ancient bones and teeth, can tell us a lot about animals that lived a long time ago. By comparing these fossils to the skeletons of animals that are alive today, we can get a good idea of an animal's size and shape, how it moved, and what kinds of food it ate. In a few rare fossils, the imprint of skin, scales or feathers is preserved. Fossils, however, can't tell us what colour an animal was or whether it had spots, stripes or other patterns. A small plant-eating animal that lived among the trees, like a present-day deer, was probably a dull colour to help it blend in with its environment. A hunting animal that lived on the open plains may have been the colour of dry grass, like a modern-day African lion. A predator that stalked its prey in the forest could have had stripes like a tiger that helped to camouflage it. Other animals may have attracted mates or signalled others of their kind with patches of bright colour, like many modern birds and lizards. The patterns and colours of the animals in this book are best guesses based on how ancient animals lived and on the appearance of modern animals that live the same way.

Morganucodon (*mor*-gan-*u*-co-don), which means "Morgan's tooth," was a primitive mammal that lived 200 million years ago. It was small, with a body only about ten centimetres long. Its large eyes suggest that it was active at night, which would have helped it hide from the many predatory reptiles and dinosaurs that lived at the same time. "Morgan's tooth" probably had a keen sense of smell, and it fed on insects and worms.

Velociraptor (vee-*lohs*-i-*rap*-tor) was a quick and aggressive predatory dinosaur that lived about 75 million years ago. It had sharp fangs and claws, with a special "killing claw" several centimetres long on each back foot. It was a fast runner that probably

hunted in packs. Though small for a dinosaur – only about two metres long and weighing around 14 kilograms – several *Velociraptors* working together could bring down prey much larger than themselves. Recently, many scientists who study dinosaurs have suggested that *Velociraptor* and other birdlike dinosaurs were covered with feathers, probably to help them keep warm.

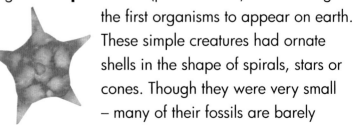

Single-celled **protozoa** (pro-toh-*zoh*-a) were among the first organisms to appear on earth. These simple creatures had ornate shells in the shape of spirals, stars or cones. Though they were very small – many of their fossils are barely visible to the naked eye – their shells accumulated on the ocean floor in unimaginable numbers, where time and pressure gradually turned them into limestone. In some parts of the world, as mountains were formed and continents shifted, the ocean floor was lifted high above the water. In these places the fossilised skeletons of these tiny creatures can be seen today as limestone cliffs hundreds of metres tall.

Diplocaulus (*dip*-lo-*cawl*-us), an aquatic animal 90 centimetres long. It had large winglike horns that might have acted as fins, helping the animal glide through the water. These horns might also have helped protect *Diplocaulus* from predators by making it hard to swallow.

The **sea scorpion** was one of the top predators of its time. It hunted fish and other small animals in warm, shallow seas some 420 million years ago. This ancestor of the lobster grew to be two metres long. It had good eyesight and large clawlike fangs. Some sea scorpions were able to breathe air and could climb on to the land.

The largest insect that ever lived was an ancient relative of the **dragonfly.** It hunted some 300 million years ago in the forests of what is now Europe. With wings nearly 70 centimetres across, it was a frightening aerial predator. Like a modern dragonfly, it was a speedy flier that could change direction quickly, grabbing smaller insects out of the air and eating them on the wing.

Many early fish, such as the **spiny shark,** were heavily armoured to protect them from larger predators. This small meat eater, about the size of a pet goldfish, appeared about 410 million years ago. Armoured fish, some the size of a bus, would swim in the earth's seas, rivers and lakes for the next 170 million years.

Three hundred million years ago the dominant animals on earth were amphibians, the ancestors of today's frogs and salamanders. Some of these animals were sharp-toothed hunters over three metres long. Others looked like eels or snakes. One of the oddest was

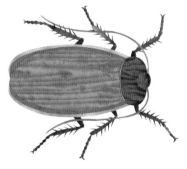

The **cockroach** is one of the oldest living animals. Cockroaches of one kind or another have been around for more than 300 million years. Some of these early cockroaches were huge – up to 10 centimetres long. They lived in warm, swampy fern forests.

Arthropods are animals with hard-shelled, jointed bodies, such as insects, crabs, scorpions and centipedes. They are a very ancient group of animals that first appeared more than 500 million years ago. The largest arthropod ever to live on land was a giant **millipede** that lived about 300 million years ago. It grew to two metres long, and probably burrowed into the forest floor, feeding on decaying plant material.

Dinocephalosaurus (*di*-no-*sef*-ah-lo-*sawr*-us), which means "terrible-headed lizard," hunted fish in warm, shallow seas about 230 million years ago. Its neck was more than twice as long as its body. Overall, it was about two and a half metres in length. This reptile's head, perched at the end of its long neck, would have looked like just another small fish as it approached its prey in murky water. When it was close enough, *Dinocephalosaurus* was able to quickly expand its throat and suck up its unlucky victim.

Not all dinosaurs were big. **Saltopus** (*salt*-oh-pus) was a birdlike animal that ran on two long legs. It weighed about one kilogram – the same as a large squirrel. *Saltopus* lived 210 million years ago, and was one of the first dinosaurs to appear. It used its

speed and needle-sharp teeth to catch and eat insects and other small animals.

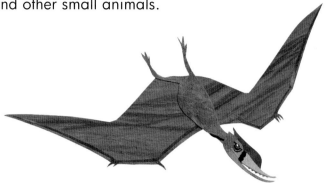

Flying reptiles, or pterosaurs (*ter*-o-sawrs), first appeared about 215 million years ago. As a group, they survived for the next 150 million years. Some were the size of a small bird. Others were gigantic, with wings 11 metres across. **Dsungaripterus** (*jung*-ah-*rip*-ter-us) was a medium-sized pterosaur, with leathery wings three metres wide, that lived about 135 million years ago. Its fossils are often found on the shores of what were once lakes and seas, where these flying predators may have nested and raised their young in colonies. *Dsungaripterus* had a curved beak with strong, blunt teeth, probably used for catching, prying open and crushing crabs and shellfish. The crest on this reptile's head may have been used to signal a mate. Perhaps the crest was brightly coloured, like the mating displays of many present-day reptiles and birds.

Baryonyx (*bar*-ee-*on*-iks) was one of the only dinosaurs known to eat fish. This 1,800-kilogram predator lived about 125 million years ago. Compared to other large predatory dinosaurs that walked on their back legs, *Baryonyx* was unusual. It had long jaws, like a crocodile. Instead of tiny front arms, *Baryonyx* had large arms with huge, sharp thumb claws that helped it grasp its slippery prey. All of these adaptations made *Baryonyx* very effective at catching fish.

Giganotosaurus (*jig*-ah-*not*-o-*sawr*-us), perhaps the largest land predator that has ever lived, stalked the plains of South America 100 million years ago. This dinosaur looked like a bigger, heavier version of the more familiar *Tyrannosaurus rex*. It was 14 metres long and may have weighed as much as 7,250 kilograms. At this size, it could attack even huge 90,000-kilogram plant-eating dinosaurs.

Protoceratops (*pro*-toh-*ser*-a-tops) was a plant eater with a big head, a sharp beak and a bony frill around its neck. We don't know if *Protoceratops* took care of its babies when they hatched or if they were left to fend for themselves. Though it wasn't a large dinosaur, *Protoceratops* could defend itself with its armour and its pointed beak. It was about 180 centimetres long and lived around 80 million years ago.

Leptictidium (*lep*-tik-*tid*-ee-um) made its home on the forest floor about 45 million years ago, where it ate insects and other small animals. There were several different species of these mammals. The one in this book was about 60 centimetres long and could move quickly, hopping on its big back legs. *Leptictidium* had a long, flexible nose that it used to sniff out food.

For millions of years the top predators in South America were large, flightless birds. One of these fierce hunters was known as the **terror bird**. It lived until about three million years ago. The largest of the terror birds stood two and a half metres tall. It had strong feet and claws and a huge, sharp beak, and probably could run as fast as a present-day horse.

Rodents first appeared more than 50 million years ago. **Epigaulus** (ep-ee-*gaw*-lus), a North American burrowing rodent, had long claws for digging and two horns that may have been used for self-defence. *Epigaulus* was about the size of a rabbit and lived some five million years ago. A South American relative of *Epigaulus*, an enormous guinea pig the size of a rhinoceros, was the largest rodent that has ever lived.

For Robin

Published in Great Britain in 2007 by
Frances Lincoln Children's Books, 4 Torriano Mews,
Torriano Avenue, London NW5 2RZ
www.franceslincoln.com

British Library Cataloguing in Publication Data available on request

ISBN 978-1-84507-820-1

Printed in China

9 8 7 6 5 4 3 2 1

Epigaulus (ep-ee-*gaw*-lus)
was a rodent that lived
underground. It had long
claws and horns on its head.

5 million years ago
30 centimetres long